W9-BWA-030

Argentina

by Joyce Markovics

Consultant: Marjorie Faulstich Orellana, PhD
Professor of Urban Schooling
University of California, Los Angeles

BEARPORT
PUBLISHING

New York, New York

Credits

Cover, © Thiago Santos/iStock and © Rahhal/Shutterstock; TOC, © RemarkEliza/Shutterstock; 4, © sunsinger/ Shutterstock; 5T, © holgs/iStock; 5B, © Goran Bogicevic/Shutterstock; 7, © gary yim/Shutterstock; 8T, © Galyna Andrushko/Shutterstock; 8B, © pawopa3336/iStock; 9, © vgabusi/iStock; 10L, © cristiani/iStock; 10–11, © Foto 4440/Shutterstock; 12T, © CarGe/iStock; 12B, © Nnehring/iStock; 13, © Lauzla/iStock; 14, © De Agostini Picture Library/G. Dagli Orti/Bridgeman Images; 15, © anvmedia/iStock; 16, © Diego Grandi/Shutterstock; 17T, © travelstock44/Alamy; 17B, © Diana Golysheva/Shutterstock; 18T, © LAIF/Redux Pictures; 18B, © Brizardh/ Dreamstime; 19, © Bernardo Galmarini/Alamy; 20, © GoGo Images Corporation/Alamy; 21, © sunsinger/ Shutterstock; 22T, © Grafissimo/iStock; 22B, © Deboraht Suarez/Shutterstock; 23, © yasuhiro amano/ Shutterstock; 24, © Celso Pupo Rodrigues/Dreamstime; 25T, © CP DC Press/Shutterstock; 25B, © Bertrand Rieger/hemis/AGE Fotostock; 26, © Hervé Hughes/hemis/Alamy; 27, © Tita.ti/Shutterstock; 28L, © Ben Girardi/ Aurora Photos/Alamy; 28–29, © Igor Alecsander/iStock; 30T, © Alexandr Vorobev/Shutterstock and © Vitoria Holdings LLC/Shutterstock; 30B, © Elisa Manzati/Shutterstock; 31 (T to B), © nicolamargaret/iStock, © Ewa Studio/Shutterstock, © anvmedia/iStock, © FrankvandenBergh/iStock, and © Noblige/iStock; 32, © neftali/ Shutterstock.

Publisher: Kenn Goin
Senior Editor: Joyce Tavolacci
Creative Director: Spencer Brinker
Design: Debrah Kaiser
Photo Researcher: Thomas Persano

Library of Congress Cataloging-in-Publication Data

Names: Markovics, Joyce L., author.
Title: Argentina / by Joyce Markovics.
Description: New York, New York : Bearport Publishing, 2019. | Series:
   Countries we come from | Includes bibliographical references and index.
Identifiers: LCCN 2018009269 (print) | LCCN 2018009559 (ebook) |
   ISBN 9781684027354 (ebook) | ISBN 9781684026890 (library)
Subjects: LCSH: Argentina—Juvenile literature.
Classification: LCC F2808.2 (ebook) | LCC F2808.2 .M37 2019 (print) |
   DDC 982—dc23
LC record available at https://lccn.loc.gov/2018009269

For more information, write to Bearport Publishing Company, Inc., 45 West 21st Street, Suite 3B, New York, New York 10010. Printed in the United States of America.

10 9 8 7 6 5 4 3 2 1

Contents

STRIKING

LIVELY

Colorful

Argentina is a **vast** country.

It stretches to the tip of South America.

It's the eighth-largest country in the world!

Over 44 million people live in Argentina.

7

There's every kind of landscape in Argentina.

You can see mountains, forests, and deserts.

Aconcagua

Aconcagua is Argentina's tallest mountain. It's the highest point in South America!

The country also has grasslands.
This flat land is called the Pampas.

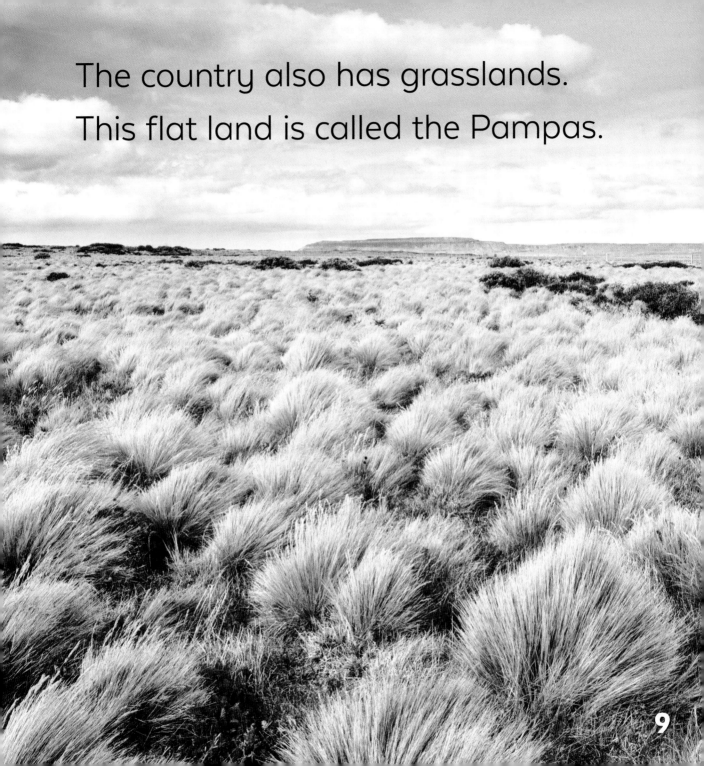

Farmers raise millions of cattle on the Pampas.

The cattle **graze** on the tall grasses.

Cowboys, called gauchos, care for the animals.

a gaucho with his horse

Farmers also grow wheat, soybeans, and corn on the Pampas.

Many wild animals call Argentina home.

Giant condors fly in the sky.

Elephant seals relax along the coast.

Andean condor

elephant seal

Guanacos (gwah-NAH-kohz) roam Argentina. These animals look like llamas.

13

Argentina has a long history.

Native people have lived there for thousands of years.

The Spanish arrived in 1516.

The Spanish ruled Argentina for 300 years.

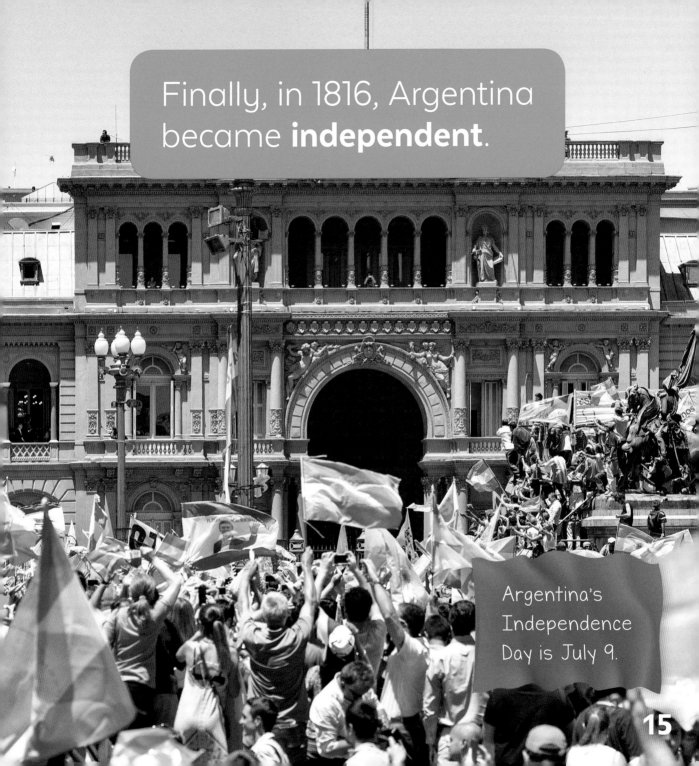

Finally, in 1816, Argentina became **independent**.

Argentina's Independence Day is July 9.

15

There are many big cities in Argentina.

The largest one is Buenos Aires.

It's also the country's **capital**!

Around 14 million people live in Buenos Aires.

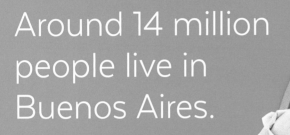

There's a park in the city that's home to hundreds of cats.

In Buenos Aires, people stroll around La Recoleta Cemetery.

It's so big that it looks like a small city!

a tomb in the cemetery

Many of the **tombs** are works of art.

La Recoleta Cemetery covers 14 acres (5.7 hectares). That's almost the size of 11 football fields!

Spanish is Argentina's main language.

This is how you say *welcome* in Spanish:

Bienvenidos
(bee-en-vuh-NEE-dos)

This is how you say *flower*:

Flor
(FLOR)

a huge flower sculpture
in Buenos Aires

Buenos Aires means
"good weather" in Spanish.

Argentina is famous for its food.

A favorite meal is *parrillada* (pahr-ee-YAH-da), or barbecue.

Argentinians love fruit. They eat more fruit than any other group of people in the world!

People also enjoy *empanadas* (em-puh-NAH-duhz).

These little pies are stuffed with cheese, vegetables, or meat.

23

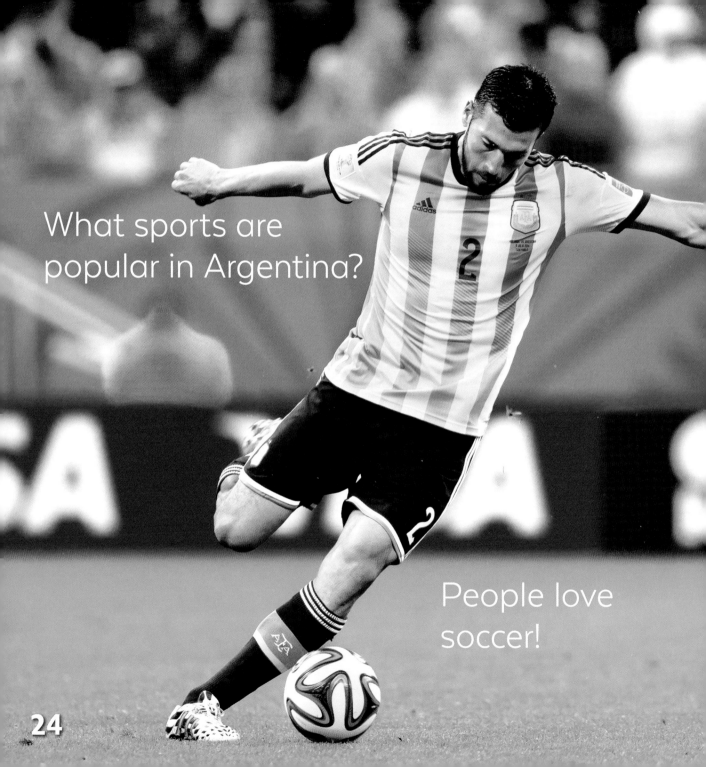

What sports are popular in Argentina?

People love soccer!

24

Fans go wild for their favorite teams.

Polo is another popular sport. It's played on horseback!

The Argentine tango is a famous dance.

Couples move their feet quickly.

They spin, leap, then hold special positions.

accordion

Tango is also a type of music. It's often played with a guitar, violins, and an accordion.

The dancers are breathtaking.

Over 5 million people visit Argentina each year.

Iguazú (ee-gwah-ZOO) Falls is a stunning spot.

The waterfalls are among the biggest in the world!

Cerro Catedral is a ski resort in the south. It draws many visitors.

Iguazú Falls

Fast Facts

Capital city:
Buenos Aires

Population of Argentina:
Over 44 million

Main language:
Spanish

Money: Argentine peso

Major religion:
Roman Catholic

Neighboring countries include:
Chile, Bolivia, Paraguay, Brazil, and
Uruguay

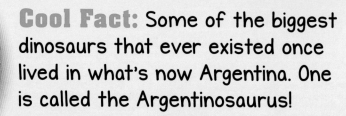

Cool Fact: Some of the biggest dinosaurs that ever existed once lived in what's now Argentina. One is called the Argentinosaurus!

Glossary

capital (KAP-uh-tuhl) a city where a country's government is based

graze (GRAYZ) to feed on plants

independent (in-di-PEN-duhnt) free from outside control

native (NAY-tiv) born in a particular place

tombs (TOOMZ) rooms, buildings, or graves where dead bodies are kept

vast (VAST) huge in size

Index

Read More

Kalman, Bobbie. *Spotlight on Argentina (Spotlight on My Country).* New York: Crabtree (2013).

Schuetz, Kari. *Argentina (Exploring Countries).* Minneapolis, MN: Bellwether (2012).

Learn More Online

To learn more about Argentina, visit
www.bearportpublishing.com/CountriesWeComeFrom

About the Author

Joyce Markovics loves exploring La Recoleta Cemetery under a moonlit sky. She'd like to dedicate this book to Michael Paul, a young adventurer.